GOAL!

The Fire and Fury of Soccer's Greatest Moment

Mark Stewart and Mike Kennedy

M MILLBROOK PRESS · MINNEAPOLIS

The following images were provided by the Authors: Authors' Collection, pp. 13, 23 (bottom), 27 (top), 53, 59; Editions Rencontre S.A., pp. 17 (top), 19 (top), 58 (top); Futera FZ, LLC, p. 17 (bottom); Fax-Pax Ltd., pp. 19 (bottom), 29 (top); Panini S.P.A., pp. 21 (top), 23 (top), 31 (bottom), 35 (bottom), 39; Country & Sporting Publications, Ltd., pp. 21 (bottom), 40; Match, p. 25 (top); Longacre Press, pp. 25 (bottom), 27 (bottom); Venorlandus, Ltd., p. 29 (bottom); The Upper Deck Co., pp. 31 (top), 33 (top); Roox Sports, p. 33 (bottom); Brooke Bond & Company, p. 35 (top); Gallaher Ltd., p. 37; Editorial GPCB, p. 38; A&BC, p. 42; IPC Magazines, Ltd., p. 45; GO Magazine, Ltd., p. 51.

The following images are used with the permission of: © Albert Moldvay/National Geographic/Getty Images, p. 4; © Rischgitz/Getty Images, p. 6; © Popperfoto/Getty Images, pp. 9, 12, 18, 20, 22, 26; © Martin Rose/Bongrats/Getty Images, pp. 10, 11, 14 (background), 51 (background), 54 (background), 56 (background), 57; © Jed Jacobsohn/Getty Images, p. 14; © Bob Thomas/Popperfoto/Getty Images, p. 16; © Rolls Press/Popperfoto/Getty Images, p. 24; © Bob Thomas/Getty Images, pp. 28, 30, 41, 44; © Vincent Laforet/Getty Images, p. 32; © Gary M. Prior/Getty Images, p. 34; © Allsport UK/Getty Images, p. 43; © Damien Meyer/AFP/Getty Images, p. 47; © Jonathan Daniel/Getty Images, p. 48; © Cristina Quicler/AFP/Getty Images, p. 50; © Chris Trotman/Getty Images for the New York Red Bulls, p. 54; © AFP/Getty Images, p. 56; © Patrick Hertzog/AFP/Getty Images, p. 58 (bottom); © Marcus Brandt/AFP/Getty Images, p. 60; © Chris Coleman/Manchester United via Getty Images, p. 61; © Filippo Monteforte/AFP/Getty Images, p. 62.

Front Cover: © Larsen, Haakon Mosvold/AFP/Getty Images. Front Cover Flap: © Bob Thomas/Getty Images (left); © Popperfoto/Getty Images (right).

Special thanks to Ben Gould, Mike Jacobsen, Susan Wade & Danny Peters

Millbrook Press
A division of Lerner Publishing Group, Inc.
241 First Avenue North
Minneapolis, MN 55401 U.S.A.

Website address: www.lernerbooks.com

Library of Congress Cataloging-in-Publication Data

Stewart, Mark.
    Goal : the fire and fury of soccer's greatest moment / by Mark Stewart and Mike Kennedy.
       p.   cm.
    Includes index.
    ISBN: 978–0–8225–8754–5 (lib. bdg. : alk. paper)
    1. Soccer—Goalkeeping. 2. Soccer—Defense. I. Kennedy, Mike. II. Title.
    GV943.9.G62S74 2010
    796.334'26—dc22   2009014098

Manufactured in the United States of America
1 – DP – 12/15/2009

Contents

Introduction 4

1   **Kicking Back**—THE STORY OF SOCCER 6

2   **History in the Making**—TEN GREAT GOALS 15

3   **Finishers**—THE ART OF THE GOAL 36

4   **Did You See That?**—AMAZING GOALS AND GOAL SCORERS 49

5   **A Little Help!**—
THE WEIRDEST, WILDEST GOALS IN SOCCER HISTORY 55

6   **For the Record**—WORLD CUP GOAL-SCORING RECORDS 58

7   **Back of the Net**—THE FUTURE OF THE GOAL 61

Resources 63

Index 64

Introduction

Right now, somewhere in the world, a soccer team and its fans are celebrating. What has caused this outburst of emotion? Someone has just sent the ball to the back of the net and scored a goal. There is no greater achievement in soccer.

Goal scorers come in all shapes and sizes. They may be girls and boys on a youth league team in the United States. Perhaps they are Chinese factory workers on their lunch break. Might they be teenagers kicking the ball on a beach in Brazil? Or professional stars playing in Italy with 100,000 fans cheering them on?

Regardless of where soccer is played or who is playing it, all players share a common bond. They try their best to score a goal, while also working as a team to prevent their opponents from scoring. That is why soccer has been called a game with two halves. When the ball is in play, everyone on the field has to think about offense and defense at the same time. No wonder goals are so hard to score!

This book looks at what it takes to score a goal. It shows the many different ways that goals are scored. Of course, there is much more to soccer than kicking or heading the ball into the net. But to truly grasp the heart of the sport, it is important to understand the magic, the mystery, and the magnificence of that amazing moment when everything comes together perfectly for a goal.

Soccer's most famous goal scorer, Pelé, celebrates after scoring against Italy in Aztec Stadium in Mexico. Pelé's talent and creativity made him the game's most beloved player.

1 Kicking Back

THE STORY OF SOCCER

Who scored the first soccer goal? That person's name has been lost to history. What we do know is that for thousands of years humans have played games that involve kicking a ball. In the ancient cultures of Mexico and Central America, these types of games were a very important part of everyday life. More than 1,000 ball courts have been discovered by archaeologists. Some are more than 3,000 years old.

The object of ancient kicking games was to keep a ball in the air and then return it to the opposing team. Players were allowed to use any part of the body except the hands. These games were kind of like a combination of volleyball and Hacky Sack. The Aztec and Mayan people added stone rings to the side of the court. If a player could direct the ball through a ring, his team automatically won the game. Some say this was the first opportunity to score a "goal."

In the 1500s, Spanish explorers were amazed by this game. They brought players back across the Atlantic Ocean to demonstrate it for King Charles I. The king and his court were more amazed by the ball than by the players. The

Soccer in early times was a rough game. As this 1754 print from Great Britain shows, it was often played on the main street of a town instead of a field.

ball was made of rubber, which was unknown to Europeans at the time. The ball bounced unlike anything they had ever seen or imagined. Religious leaders were convinced that the devil was responsible for the ball's odd behavior! They forbid the game to be shown to the public.

In England another game also caused concern. It was a rough and rowdy sport that came to be known as foot-ball. Players kicked one another as often as they kicked the ball. A game might begin in a town square, but it often spilled into the surrounding streets. It destroyed everything in its path. King Edward III wanted his young subjects to practice archery and swordsmanship instead of foot-ball. England needed soldiers, not foot-ball players! He wasn't happy when they were injured booting a ball back and forth. Edward III outlawed foot-ball in the 1300s. Several kings after him also banned the game.

Foot-ball had come to the British Isles more than a thousand years earlier. Back then the land was part of the Roman Empire. Roman soldiers played the game to relieve boredom and improve their footwork. When the Romans left, the game was kept alive by the Celtic people of Ireland, Wales, and Scotland. Entire villages would split into two teams and kick an object back and forth across a field after the harvest was done. Was this meant to represent the sun crossing the field? Many people believe that it was.

A game similar to foot-ball was played in China and Japan for many centuries. The Chinese called it kick-ball. Kicking games were also popular among the native people of the South Pacific and North America. Indeed, when the first colonists arrived in America, they were amazed to find people playing a very familiar game. It looked just like the one that was so frowned upon back in England.

Foot-ball almost died out in England. It lived on at a handful of schools in the early 1800s. Most of the pupils at these schools were the sons of important families. These children would one day have to run the rapidly growing British Empire. For this reason, the school headmasters believed it was important for

Young Englishmen play a soccer game during the late 1800s. Notice that there is no net behind the goal.

their students to learn how to work together. Playing a team sport was a great way to develop this skill.

When these same wealthy young men went off to college, they brought football with them. However, when they gathered for a game, there was often a problem. Each student had learned the game according to different rules. At some schools, players had been allowed to use their hands and feet. At others, players could only use their feet.

The college students needed to agree on a single set of rules. After much debate, the game was divided into different sports—rugby and football. Rugby was a carrying and tackling game. Football—the game called soccer in North America—was a dribbling and kicking game with very little body-to-body contact.

What's in a Name?

In 1863 the Football Association was started by a group of players in England. In 1871 the Rugby Football Union began. To avoid confusion, the games were called association football and rugby football. Young men at the time liked to create nicknames by taking the first syllable of a word and adding –er to it. Thus rugby football became "rugger." That didn't really work for association football, so the second syllable of "association" was used. That is how the name "soccer" came to be.

By the end of the 1800s, soccer had become the most popular sport in Great Britain. Thanks to the Football Association (FA), there were teams in almost every town and city. Each year, they competed for the FA Cup. Some teams used amateurs. Others hired professional players. Many relied on a combination. By the 1890s, all the top English teams were professional. Soccer was watched and played by members of all the social classes. The best players were well-paid. Fans cared only about winning. It did not matter to them whether the star of their team was the son of a coal miner or the son of a politician. Soccer had become a "game of the people."

Soccer reached other parts of the world thanks to Englishmen who had played the game as schoolboys. They went to different countries in Europe, Africa, and the Americas to seek their fortunes as engineers, bankers, merchants, and army officers. Being so far away from home, they formed social clubs with other Englishmen. For exercise, they played soccer. The people around them watched in wonder. Soon they were playing too. By the early 1900s, dozens of nations had caught the fever.

One country where soccer did not catch on right away was the United States. The game's popularity in the United States rose and fell during the late-1800s and early 1900s. Why did this happen when the rest of the world was so crazy about soccer? For a long time, Americans rejected British ideas and customs. Soccer first came to the United States with immigrants from Great Britain, so many people did not want to play it.

Where soccer was played in the United States, it often was viewed as a working-class game, instead of a game for everyone. It thrived in factory towns in the Northeast. It was popular in some midwestern cities, including Saint Louis. The game was also played by immigrant workers in the Southwest. Eventually, schoolchildren began to play. Some colleges adopted the sport too. Professional and semiprofessional leagues popped up from time to time. But while soccer in other countries was growing and improving very quickly, it was slow to develop in the United States.

During the 1920s, soccermania gripped the planet like never before. The end of World War I (1914–1918) and social changes that swept Europe and the Americas meant people had more time for recreation and to go to sporting events. In many European and Latin American countries, soccer was the game they chose.

People liked soccer because the rules were very basic. It was easy for fans to understand. Players did not have to buy expensive equipment. And there was something else that made soccer a popular global sport. Each country's athletes gave the game a different flavor, or "personality." The sport truly reflected a nation's style. This is still true today.

The Offside

In soccer a referee can call a team offside if a player is nearer to an opponent's goalkeeper than the ball and one other defender. This is to keep players from "hanging" in back of the defense, where it would be much easier to score goals. To be onside, a player must make sure that there is always a defender in front of him until the ball arrives.

During the 1800s and early 1900s, the offside rule was much stricter than it is today. It said that two defenders had to be between a player and the goalkeeper. This was sometimes called the Three-Man Rule. It was very difficult for a player to keep track of two defenders and the ball. Often, defenders worked together to "trap" opponents into stepping offside just before receiving a pass.

This slowed the game down and made it very dull. In 1925 the offside rule was changed to the present one. Not surprisingly, goal scoring soared until defenses found ways to adjust their tactics.

The Bolton Wanderers and West Ham United play in the 1923 FA Cup Final in England's Wembley Stadium. Bolton won 2–0.

The growing passion for soccer came at an especially good time for the sport. In much of the world during the 1920s, working people had more money in their pockets. Eight-hour workdays meant they also had more free time on their hands. They attended matches in great numbers. A crowd of 5,000 spectators had been remarkable before World War I. After the war, crowds of 30,000 or more often pressed into stadiums for important games. A ticket to a soccer match was an excellent way for people to escape from their troubles for a few hours.

The skill level of soccer around the world grew quickly. In fact, it became good enough to hold a global tournament. In 1930 the World Cup was created by the Fédération Internationale de Football Association (FIFA). The South American country of Uruguay hosted the first World Cup. FIFA planned to hold it every four years. (It has done so, except in 1942 and 1946 when the tournament was suspended because of World War II.) World Cup soccer remained popular even in years when there was no tournament. Countries had to play one another just to earn a spot in the tournament.

After the first World Cup in 1930, scoring a goal in the international tournament was viewed as the crowning moment in a player's career. It made his name known throughout the soccer world—and often turned him into a national hero. If a player scored the goal that won the championship final, fans remembered his name forever.

In 1958 World Cup matches were broadcast around the world on television for the first time. Most fans in Europe believed their countries played the best brand of soccer. They soon learned otherwise. The crisp-passing, sharpshooting team from Brazil won the championship. An acrobatic teenager named Pelé led Brazil. Millions of people who had never followed the sport closely were amazed by Pelé. They became lifelong soccer fans.

In the 1960s and 1970s, soccer became a truly global sport. Even the United States was now on board. At American high schools and colleges, players learned the fine points of the game. A professional league—the North American Soccer League (NASL)—was formed. Many international stars came to the United States to finish their careers in the NASL. That included Pelé, the greatest star of them all. He believed the United States was a soccer giant waiting to be awoken. Pelé played for the New York Cosmos of the NASL. He acted as a soccer "ambassador" to the United States.

In this advertisement for the first World Cup, the words "Campeonato Mundial" mean "World Championship."

Around the rest of the world, soccer was bigger and better than ever. There were soccer tournaments held at different times throughout the year. Some were between professional clubs, and some were between national clubs. A French star might play for an Italian club or an Argentine star might play for a Spanish club. A Brazilian player and a German player might be teammates one day and then find themselves playing against each other in a tournament between their countries. Today there are more pro soccer players than in any other three sports combined.

Playing Catch Up

Because soccer got a slow start in the United States, it took a lot of hard work to catch up to other countries. No one worked harder to see the game flourish in the United States than Pelé. In 1990 his dream came true when Team USA qualified for the World Cup for the first time since 1950. In 1994 the United States hosted the World Cup. And in 1996, a strong new pro league—Major League Soccer (MLS)—began play. It showcased the talent of American college stars Tony Meola, Alexi Lalas, John Harkes, Cobi Jones, Chris Henderson, Jeff Cunningham, Taylor Twellman, and others.

Also during the 1990s, women's soccer took off. The U.S. team stormed to the top of the world rankings. American stars such as

Michelle Akers, Mia Hamm (*at left, with teammates*), Kristine Lilly, and Julie Foudy were considered among the best in the world. At the college level, coach Anson Dorrance built a powerhouse team at the University of North Carolina. The United States won the Women's World Cup in 1991 and 1999, and Olympic gold medals in 1996, 2004, and 2008. The United States hosted the Women's World Cup in 1999 and again in 2003.

Women's soccer in the United States had an advantage that men's soccer did not. The men's game started slowly and lagged behind the rest of the world. Women's soccer did not become popular around the world until the 1980s, so all countries started off even.

What is it that people find so wonderful about soccer? It is a simple game. A goal is worth one point. The only way to score is to propel the ball past the goalkeeper without using your hands. At the same time, soccer can be very complicated. Watching a game is like peeking inside a car engine. All the parts move together, with and against one another. It is exciting to see the game played at its highest level.

Another great part of watching soccer is the explosion of joy when a goal is scored. The players on the field go crazy. The stands shake under the weight of the cheering crowd. Of all the amazing things about the game, perhaps the most amazing thing is that just when you think you've seen it all, something happens that you've never seen before!

2 History in the Making

TEN GREAT GOALS

Scoring a goal is a thrill for anyone who has ever stepped onto a soccer field. Whether the play is the result of perfectly executed teamwork or simply good luck, nothing beats the feeling of watching the ball ruffle the back of the net.

Of course, the bigger the game and the more tense the moment, the more dramatic the goal becomes. What then makes a truly great goal? Soccer fans have been debating this question for a century or more. If your team scores, every goal is great! The truly special ones, however, combine the best that soccer has to offer.

A great goal must be scored at a crucial time, in a meaningful game, by an important player. It must come on a magnificent or unusual shot. And it must change the course of history in some way.

How many goals fall into this category? Again, this is another question that soccer fans love to debate. Everyone has a different opinion. This chapter tells the stories of ten unforgettable goals and the people who played a part in making them great.

Italy's Orsi Spins a Winning Tale

The 1930 World Cup was held in Uruguay. It was a contest of South American powers. Four years later, the World Cup was held in Italy. It turned into a contest of European powers. In the semifinals, Czechoslovakia beat Germany and the host country, Italy, beat Austria. That set up a final game between Czechoslovakia and Italy. Fans for the home team cheered wildly as their players put the pressure on Czech goalkeeper Frantisek Planicka again and again.

But no matter how hard the Italians tried, they could not get the ball past Planicka. Meanwhile, Czechoslovakia's Antonin Puc drilled the ball into Italy's goal for a 1–0 lead. There were only 20 minutes left in the game. Then the Czechs missed two chances for a second score. This gave Italy a chance. Still, time was ticking away.

With only eight minutes to go, Italy's Raimundo Orsi dribbled through the defense and prepared to take a shot. It looked as if Orsi would strike the ball with his left foot. Instead, he changed his mind and jabbed at it with his right foot. The ball spun wildly and curved suddenly as it headed

Italian players lift their coach, Vittorio Pozzo, on their shoulders after winning the 1934 World Cup.

for the goal. Planicka was fooled. The Czech keeper got a few fingers on Orsi's shot but could not stop it.

Orsi's goal saved the day for Italy. The game went into extra time tied at 1–1. Seven minutes later, Angelo Schiavio scored for the Italians. They held on for a dramatic 2–1 victory. The next day, Orsi returned to the field with a group of reporters and photographers. He tried for a half hour to make the same shot. He couldn't do it—it was truly a once-in-a-lifetime goal.

COLLECTOR'S CORNER

RAIMUNDO ORSI

Orsi was born in Argentina and played for that country in the 1928 Olympics. His Italian ancestry made him eligible to play for Italy. He helped the Italian club Juventus win five league championships in the 1930s.

1979 Sportscaster Raimundo Orsi card

FRANTISEK PLANICKA

Planicka was Europe's top goalkeeper in the 1930s. In the 1938 World Cup, he played an entire half against Brazil with a broken arm. In those days, teams were not allowed to substitute for injured players.

1998 Futera Frantisek Planicka card

Gaetjens and the United States Clean Up against England

JUNE 29, 1950 • UNITED STATES VS. ENGLAND
WORLD CUP GROUP 2 MATCH • BELO HORIZONTE, BRAZIL

The talk of the 1950 World Cup was England. The English players believed their brand of soccer was the best in the world. Yet they had never participated in the tournament before. They simply felt they had nothing to prove. In 1950 the English decided to show their skill on the world stage. England's second opponent of the World Cup was the United States. English coach Walter Winterbottom was supremely confident. Instead of making his players practice before the match, he gave them the day off.

The Americans were little more than a pickup team. One of their best players was a Haitian immigrant named Joe Gaetjens. He was in the United States studying accounting. To earn money while in school, Gaetjens washed dishes in a Brooklyn restaurant.

Early in the match, the English pounded the U.S. goal with shot after shot with no success. England's star Tom Finney had a great scoring chance, but his header was tipped away. The Americans fought back. Walter Bahr of

Bert Williams (*left*) stares in disbelief as Joe Gaetjens's header settles into the back of the net.

Fußball

WM 1950

JOE GAETJENS

Gaetjens was allowed to play for the United States because he announced that he would apply for citizenship. He never did. Gaetjens later played professional soccer in France and Haiti.

1977 Sportscaster Joe Gaetjens card

TOM FINNEY

Finney was a great striker—he could play left, right, or center forward. In the match against the United States, he had a point-blank look at the goal at the end of the first half. Time ran out just as he was about to attempt a shot.

1986 Fax-Pax Tom Finney card

the United States took a shot at the English goal from 25 yards away. Bert Williams moved to catch Bahr's shot. At the last instant, the ball ticked off Gaetjens's head—just enough to fool Williams and settle into the net.

That was the one and only goal of the day. The Americans held on to win. When British fans saw the 0–1 score afterward, they assumed it was a misprint. They thought the score must have been 10–1!

Helmut Halts Hungary

JULY 4, 1954 • WEST GERMANY VS. HUNGARY • WORLD CUP FINAL • BERNE, SWITZERLAND

When the 1954 World Cup began, no team looked good enough to beat Hungary. The Magic Magyars had it all. They had great passers and shooters, a rock-solid defense, and a brilliant coach. They played soccer faster and smarter than anyone else in the world. Hungary's leader was Ferenc Puskas. Few players could control the ball as he did. Teammates used to throw him soap in the shower, and he would catch it with his left foot!

In the opening round, Hungary destroyed West Germany 8–3. However, the West Germans won the rest of their games. They made it to the final, where they met Hungary again. This time the game was closer. The Hungarian players were tired and hurt. They had played tough games against Brazil and Uruguay. On the other hand, West Germany was fresh after an easy victory over Austria. Still, Hungary opened the game with two goals.

West German coach Sepp Herberger told his players to keep pressing the Hungarians. He was certain they would tire

Hungarian keeper Gyula Grosics cannot reach a perfectly placed shot by Helmut Rahn.

out. Herberger was right. Hungary gave up an easy goal. Seven minutes later, Helmut Rahn blasted a shot to tie the score at 2–2.

The second half was thrilling. The fans were on the edge of their seats. Hungary missed a couple of easy shots that could have won the game. Finally, with five minutes left, the exhausted Hungarians were too slow to clear a loose ball from in front of their goal. Rahn swooped in and drilled the game winner. The 3–2 victory was one of the great upsets in World Cup history.

1954 RAHN (Deutschland)

HELMUT RAHN

Rahn played in 40 international matches and scored 21 goals. He was the first player to score four goals in two different World Cups. Thanks to Rahn's heroics against Hungary, West Germany's victory is known as the Miracle of Berne.

1970 Panini Helmut Rahn card

FERENC PUSKAS

Puskas was the most feared scorer in the world during the 1950s. He was also the heart of the powerhouse Hungarian team. Puskas scored over 500 goals in his career, including 50 in 32 games during 1947–1948.

1956 *World Sports* Ferenc Puskas

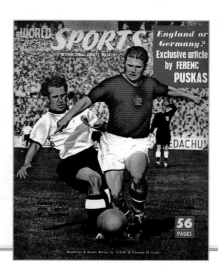

Pelé Stuns the Swedes

When Brazil brought 17-year-old Pelé to Sweden for the 1958 World Cup, fans thought coach Vincent Feola had lost his mind. Feola himself admitted that the talented teenager was not mature enough to handle the pressure. He planned to use Pelé at the end of games to give Brazil's stars a rest.

That plan changed in the quarterfinal against Wales. Pelé scored a fantastic goal, and Brazil won 1–0. Against France in the semifinal, he scored three goals in 23 minutes in the second half. That set up a final between Brazil and the home team, Sweden.

Pelé squeezes a goal past the Swedish defense in Brazil's 5–2 victory.

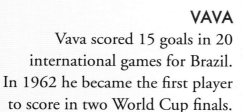

PELÉ

Pelé sat on the bench for Brazil's first two games of the 1958 World Cup, against Austria and England. Through 2006 he was still the youngest player ever to score a World Cup goal.

1970 Panini Pelé card

VAVA

Vava scored 15 goals in 20 international games for Brazil. In 1962 he became the first player to score in two World Cup finals.

Vava autographed photo

Two of Pelé's young teammates, Vava and Garrincha, gave Brazil a 2–1 lead in the first half. Early in the second half, Pelé received a high pass with his back to Sweden's goal. He stopped the ball with his chest, flipped the ball over his shoulder, and spun around his bewildered defenders. As the ball came down, Pelé was facing the goalkeeper with no one else in front of him. He blasted a shot into the net for the most fantastic goal anyone had ever seen. Brazil scored twice more to win 5–2.

Pelé's magic act had come at just the right time. The 1958 World Cup was the first to be televised around the planet. A week earlier, Pelé had been an unknown. After this game, everyone was calling him the greatest player in the world.

Hurst's Heroic Hat Trick Lifts England

In 1966 the country that boasted it had invented soccer still had not won a World Cup. So the pressure was really on England. The Brits were hosting the tournament for the first time. Coach Alf Ramsey and his players were still angry about the loss to the United States in 1950. This time England had an excellent team. It included Bobby Moore, Bobby Charlton, Martin Peters, and Alan Ball. England's only worry was goal scoring. Jimmy Greaves, a famous sharpshooter, was injured early in the tournament against France. Ramsey replaced him with Geoff Hurst.

The English advanced to the final, where they faced West Germany. The match was tense from the beginning. A generation earlier, England and Germany had been at war. Millions were killed on both sides. On the soccer field, Germany had won six of the last seven times the countries had met.

After 90 minutes, the game was tied 2–2. Although Greaves was then healthy, Ramsey kept Hurst in the lineup. Hurst had already scored a goal on a header. Peters had scored England's other goal.

England's Bobby Moore raises the Jules Rimet Trophy, which is awarded to the World Cup champion.

Ten minutes into extra time, Hurst hammered a shot at West Germany's goal. The ball slammed against the crossbar, ricocheted to the ground, and then spun back onto the field—all in a split second. Had the ball crossed the goal line? The linesman signaled that it had. The fans in Wembley Stadium went wild. Moments later, Hurst scored his third goal to notch a rare hat trick. His goal made the final score 4–2. England had its first World Cup, and Hurst became a national hero.

No. 13 Geoff Hurst
(England)

GEOFF HURST

Hurst was the first to score a hat trick in a World Cup final. He was also a talented cricket player. Hurst was knighted by Queen Elizabeth in 1998.

1986 Match Geoff Hurst card

MARTIN PETERS

Peters was one of England's best young playmakers. He played all over the field and loved to challenge enemy defenses. He was one of the few pro athletes to star in four different decades—the 1950s, 1960s, 1970s, and 1980s.

1970 *Famous Footballers* Martin Peters

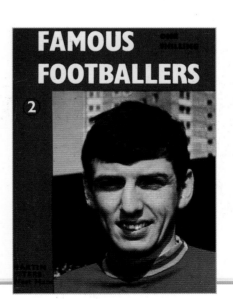

Alberto Puts the Final Stroke on Brazil's Masterpiece

JUNE 21, 1970 • BRAZIL VS. ITALY • WORLD CUP FINAL • MEXICO CITY, MEXICO

For many soccer fans, the 1970 World Cup stands out as the greatest ever—thanks mainly to Brazil. The country featured an amazing lineup of world-class players. In uniform for Brazil were Pelé, Jairzinho, Gérson, Tostão, Rivelino, Clodoaldo, and Carlos Alberto. The Brazilians blended style and skill like no team before or since.

In an opening-round match against England, Jairzinho passed to Pelé for a perfect header into the corner of the goal. Fans gasped at the beauty of their teamwork. They were equally astounded when Gordon Banks blocked the shot for one of the greatest saves in World Cup history.

Tostão and Pelé celebrate Brazil's final goal in their 1970 World Cup victory.

CARLOS ALBERTO

Alberto was the captain of the 1970 World Cup team. In 1977 he joined the New York Cosmos of the NASL. Alberto won three championships with the Cosmos.

Carlos Alberto autographed photo

PELÉ

The 1970 World Cup was Pelé's last. He retired from soccer for a while and then returned to play in the NASL as Alberto's teammate. Pelé's great dream was to popularize soccer in the United States.

Famous Footballers Pelé

Brazil advanced to the final against Italy. The Italians hoped to stop Brazil's marvelous passing by bunching up near their goal. The strategy didn't work. Pelé scored on two headers. He also headed a pass to Jairzinho for an easy goal. The final score was 4–1.

The goal that everyone remembers from this game was the final one. Six Brazilians touched the ball as the team worked its magic. The seventh player, Alberto, swept the ball past the keeper with his right foot. It was a magnificent team effort— Alberto just happened to finish the play.

Maradona Hands Argentina a Sweet Victory

JUNE 22, 1986 • ARGENTINA VS. ENGLAND
WORLD CUP QUARTERFINAL • MEXICO CITY, MEXICO

In 1984 England and Argentina went to war in the South Atlantic. They battled over the windswept Falkland Islands. Two years later, their soccer teams met in a World Cup battle. England may have won the war, but what most people remember is that Argentina won the game.

The star of Argentina's team—and the best player in the tournament—was Diego Maradona. He was a marvelous, creative player. Although Maradona had a sore knee, he was still very dangerous.

England and Argentina met in the quarterfinal. The match was scoreless in the second half when England's Steve Hodge lifted a lazy back pass to his keeper, Peter Shilton. Maradona raced toward Shilton and jumped high. He tried to head the ball into the net. As the two players collided, Maradona's hand hit the ball, which rolled into the

English keeper Peter Shilton can't leap high enough to stop Diego Maradona's illegal punched shot.

goal. The referee did not see what had happened. He ruled that the goal counted. Maradona later said it was the "hand of God" that punched the ball in!

Later in the half, Maradona dribbled the entire length of the field. He swerved around five players and scored another goal. It was an amazing play—maybe the most amazing ever in World Cup history. To this day, however, Maradona is best known for his Hand of God goal!

Diego Maradona

DIEGO MARADONA

Argentina went on to beat West Germany in the final of the 1986 World Cup. Maradona set up the winning goal with a great pass to Jorge Burruchaga. In 2008 Maradona was named coach of Argentina's national team.

1993 Fax-Pax Diego Maradona card

PETER SHILTON

Shilton's career lasted 30 years. He played in 1,237 matches—more than anyone else in the history of soccer. During the 1980s, soccer fans could buy a computer video game called *Peter Shilton's Handball Maradona*!

1980 Flik Card Peter Shilton card

PETER SHILTON

Van Basten Shoots Down the Soviets

JUNE 25, 1988 • NETHERLANDS VS. SOVIET UNION
EUROPEAN FOOTBALL CHAMPIONSHIP FINAL • MUNICH, GERMANY

The Euro 88 tournament brought together eight of the world's top national teams for 16 amazing days of soccer. Superstars Ruud Gullit and Marco Van Basten led the Netherlands. Van Basten had a sore ankle, but it didn't show when the Dutch beat England 3–1 early in the tournament. Van Basten scored all three of his team's goals.

The Netherlands faced the Soviet Union in the final. The Soviets paid close attention to Van Basten. Still, in the first half, he found himself alone for a header on the left side. The Russian defense ran to him and left Gullit alone. Van Basten headed the ball to his teammate, who then headed into the unguarded net.

Marco Van Basten shows the 1988 European Cup trophy to the crowd.

MARCO VAN BASTEN

Van Basten was named the Most Valuable Player (MVP) of Euro 88. He was World Soccer Player of the Year twice in his career. Van Basten scored 25 or more goals in a season nine times from 1983 to 1992.

1994 Upper Deck Marco Van Basten card

RUUD GULLIT

Gullit and Van Basten were teammates on AC Milan in 1988. They were joined by a third Dutch superstar, Frank Rijkaard. AC Milan won the Italian league title that season.

1996 Panini Ruud Gullit sticker

NETHERLANDS 1988

In the second half, Arnold Muhren chipped a high ball across the Soviet penalty area to Van Basten. The Dutch star had no angle to shoot. Everyone expected him to tap the ball to Gullit again. Instead, he turned and kicked a topspin volley with his left foot. The shot had to be perfect—and it was. The ball looped over Rinat Dasaev, one of the best goalkeepers in the world. Van Basten's goal gave his team a 2–0 victory. Many say it was the greatest shot ever in a championship game.

The U.S. Women Score with a Full House

JULY 10, 1999 • UNITED STATES VS. CHINA
WOMEN'S WORLD CUP FINAL • PASADENA, CALIFORNIA

At the beginning of the 1990s, very few people watched women's soccer. The U.S. team was one of the best in the world, but that was hard to tell by the small crowds that showed up at games. When Mia Hamm, Julie Foudy, Kristine Lilly, Briana Scurry, and their teammates walked onto the field for the Women's World Cup final, they could hardly believe what they saw. More than 90,000 screaming fans filled the Rose Bowl. The Rose Bowl is one of the world's largest sports arenas.

Those fans were treated to a great game. The United States played China. Team USA's defenders choked off the Chinese attack. In the first 90 minutes, China managed just two shots on goal. The Americans did not do much better. After regulation time, the score was 0–0. China pressed the attack in extra time. Liu Ailing lifted a corner kick past Scurry, and Fan Yunjie raced up to head the ball toward the wide-open net. Lilly leaped high and headed the ball away before it crossed the goal line.

Brandi Chastain and her teammates jump for joy after her game-winning goal.

After 30 scoreless minutes of extra time, the teams lined up for a shootout. Each coach chose five players to shoot from point-blank range. With Liu up, Scurry made a great save. Team USA had the final shot with the score tied 4–4. Brandi Chastain was the last shooter. She drilled the ball past Gao Hong for the win. Chastain turned and ran toward the center of the field, tore off her jersey, and dropped to her knees before disappearing under a pile of happy teammates.

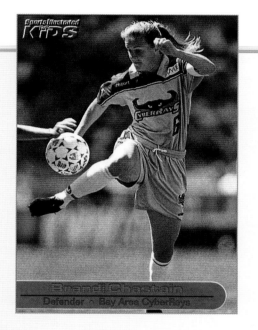

BRANDI CHASTAIN

Coach Tony DiCicco dropped Chastain from the team's shootout list after she missed a kick in an earlier loss. He played a hunch and put her back moments before the 1999 World Cup final shootout.

2002 *SI for Kids* Brandi Chastain card

BRIANA SCURRY

Scurry made the diving save that gave Team USA a chance to win the 1999 Women's World Cup. She was also the goalkeeper on the United States' gold medal Olympic teams in 1996 and 2004. Only one female keeper has played in more international matches.

1999 Roox Briana Scurry card

Zidane Zaps 'Em for the 2002 European Cup

MAY 15, 2002 • REAL MADRID VS. BAYER 04 LEVERKUSEN
CHAMPIONS LEAGUE FINAL • GLASGOW, SCOTLAND

The Champions League is a tournament that brings together the best professional teams from Europe's many leagues. It begins during the summer of one year and ends in the spring of the next. The winner gets the European Cup.

The 2002 final featured Real Madrid, a Spanish club that had won the cup eight times. Real Madrid had a galaxy of international stars. The team's lineup included Zinédine Zidane, Ronaldo, Luís Figo, Roberto Carlos, Raúl González, and David Beckham. Their opponent was Germany's Bayer 04 Leverkusen, which had never even won its own league championship. Their top players included Michael Ballack, Oliver Neuville, Lúcio, and Zé Roberto.

Zinédine Zidane (*far right*) is embraced by Real Madrid teammates after scoring his amazing goal.

ZINÉDINE ZIDANE

Zidane was a Frenchman playing for Real Madrid. He had been the star four years earlier for France in the 1998 World Cup. Zidane was named European Player of the Year three times.

2004 Brooke Bond Zinédine Zidane card

ROBERTO CARLOS

Carlos was one of the top left wings in soccer. He starred for Real Madrid for 11 seasons. The Brazilian-born wing was runner-up to Ronaldo as 1997 World Player of the Year.

2006 Panini Roberto Carlos sticker

ROBERTO CARLOS

Many saw the match as "David vs. Goliath." It proved to be a hard-fought battle. Each team scored a goal early in the game. Just before halftime, Carlos lifted a high pass to the left edge of the penalty area. Zidane turned sideways and swung his left foot. It met the ball in midair and sent a shot streaking into the top left corner of the goal. It was an absolutely perfect shot—and practically impossible to pull off! Zidane's incredible goal gave Real Madrid the lead. They hung on in a wild second half to win 2–1.

3 Finishers
THE ART OF THE GOAL

What does it take to score a goal? Strong legs, a quick mind, and a hard head. At least, that's a good start. Players must also be aware of their surroundings. Are teammates close by? How is the defense set up? The top players think a couple of passes ahead. They try to arrive in scoring position at the same time as the ball. If all goes well, the result is a clear shot at the goal. Then it is a matter of making a good, accurate shot in the split-second before the opportunity is lost.

Being a great goal scorer—putting the ball in the net game after game—takes something more than these skills. It takes creativity. It takes personality. It takes style. This chapter looks at some of soccer's best "finishers" and examines what made them great. The players are listed along with their home countries and the years they played at the first-division level.

Steve Bloomer/England   1892–1914

Goal scorers are often called marksmen, snipers, or sharpshooters. They know when to "pull the trigger" on a scoring chance. Steve Bloomer was soccer's first marksman. He played inside forward and was very good at controlling the ball. When a pass came his way, Bloomer could dribble quickly around a defender. Often, this left him face-to-face with the goalkeeper. From there, his strong and accurate shot got the job done. Bloomer was soccer's first great international star. In 23 games for England, he scored 28 goals. Many of these goals came against England's biggest rival, Scotland. Forever after, Bloomer was known as the "Hammer of the Scots."

Arthur Friedenreich/Brazil   *1909-1935*

Looking at Brazil's team today, it is hard to imagine that soccer was once an "all-white" sport in that country. But for many years, players with dark skin were not welcome on the top clubs. Arthur Friedenreich was the man who broke Brazil's color barrier. He was the son of a German immigrant father. His mother was Brazilian, of African descent. Friedenreich began playing for top clubs in Brazil as a teenager. His career lasted until he was 43. Friedenreich averaged a goal a game and was the first player to score more than 1,000 goals. At a time when soccer was mostly a defensive battle, Friedenreich was always on the lookout for an opening. When he saw one, he used his speed and aggressiveness to pounce. Not surprisingly, opponents called him the Tiger.

DIXIE DEAN

Dixie Dean was the king of goal scorers during the 1920s.

Dixie Dean/England   *1923-1939*

When soccer's offside rule was changed in the 1920s, fans knew they would see more goals. Everyone asked the same question: who would score them? The first player to take full advantage of the new rule was Bill "Dixie" Dean. In his first season, while still a teenager, he scored 27 goals in 27 games for the Tranmere Rovers. In 1927–1928, at the age of 21, Dean netted 60 goals for Everton. England's national team was quick to offer him a spot. The young forward scored 12 times in his first five matches for England.

Silvio Piola/Italy 1929–1954

During a soccer match, there are many moments when the action slows down. This gives the players a moment to catch their breaths. At these times, Silvio Piola was most dangerous. He was a tremendous athlete who could go from standing still to a full-on attack in a stride or two. Piola was a tall, strong, aggressive player who never gave up on a ball. He scored 30 goals in 24 international matches for Italy during the 1930s. Piola made soccer the country's most popular sport.

Leonidas da Silva/Brazil 1931–1950

Leonidas da Silva was soccer's first "artistic" goal scorer. He covered the field the way a painter covers a canvas. He was a fantastic dribbler and passer. He could launch a shot on goal at any time. Leonidas is given credit for inventing two of soccer's most fantastic plays, the bicycle kick and the banana kick. The truth is that others had experimented with these shots. Leonidas just turned them into deadly weapons. During the 1930s, the lightning-quick forward was the most famous star in South America. He was nicknamed Diamante Negro (Black Diamond) because he was such a rare and precious player. His fame continued long after he retired. Leonidas inspired the creation of a popular soccer-playing comic-book superhero named Diamante Negro in the 1960s and 1970s. And to this day, one of the most popular candy bars in Brazil also uses this name.

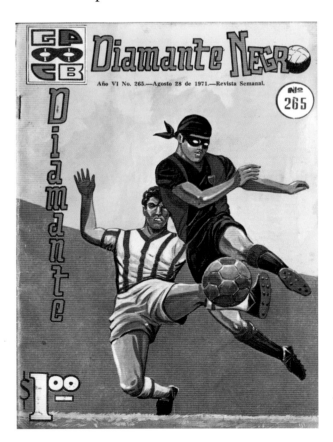

A comic book featuring Diamante Negro

Sandor Kocsis/Hungary   1943-1965

Sandor Kocsis

Winning balls in the air—especially near the goal—can change the course of a game. Sandor Kocsis was the first player who turned this skill into an art. He was called King of the Header. Kocsis could outjump the defense, keeping one eye on the ball and the other on the players around him. He would then direct the ball off his head at different speeds and angles—either into the goal or to a wide-open teammate. His finest performance came during the 1954 World Cup. He led all scorers with 11 goals in that tournament. In 68 international matches for Hungary, Kocsis scored 75 times.

Alfredo Di Stéfano/Argentina-Colombia/Spain   1943-1966

Until Pelé came along, many experts believed that Alfredo Di Stéfano was the greatest player of all time. He was certainly the most physically fit player of his era. This helped him become the game's first "two-way" star. Di Stéfano was a superb defensive player. He was like an extra fullback. But in the blink of an eye, he could lead the charge in the other direction with a perfect pass—or swoop in and finish off an attack with a beautiful goal. Di Stéfano's most amazing skill was setting up himself for goals. Instead of taking difficult shots, he often gave the ball to a teammate so he could get it into better position. Di Stéfano grew up on a farm in Argentina and played in South America during the 1940s. In the 1950s, he starred for Real Madrid in Spain. There he teamed with Ferenc Puskas to help his club win the European championship each year from 1956 to 1960.

Ferenc Puskas/Hungary-Spain   1943-1966

Hungary lost only once from 1950 to 1956. The captain of those teams was Ferenc Puskas. He was known for his powerful and accurate left-footed shot. In fact, no other player in history had a stronger left foot. Puskas was the most dangerous goal scorer of the 1950s. During his long career, he scored more often in international matches than all but one player, Pelé. What made Puskas remarkable was that he could not shoot with his right foot, and he wasn't very good at heading the ball either. In other words, everyone on the field knew what he was going to do! Puskas fled Communist Hungary in 1956 and became a Spanish citizen. He finished his career with Real Madrid in the Spanish League. In the 1960 European Cup final, Puskas scored four goals to beat Eintracht Frankfurt 7–3.

Bobby Charlton shows off his booming right leg.

Bobby Charlton/England   1954–1975

Few players have ever been as good at making long shots and passes as Bobby Charlton. As a teenager, he scored twice in his first game for Manchester United. He played on the wing for several seasons, scoring goals with his cannonlike shot. Later, he moved back to midfield. There his leadership skills helped England win its first World Cup, in 1966. Charlton's talent for scoring goals—and stopping them—made him one of the most valuable players in the history of the game.

Pelé/Brazil   1956–1977

In most sports, fans argue endlessly over which athlete was the best ever. In soccer there is nearly total agreement: Edison Arantes do Nascimento—or Pelé, as the world knows him. As a goal scorer, no one was better. Pelé could "read" goalkeepers and then quickly determine the best way to get the ball past them. He could control the speed, spin, and placement of his kicks with either foot. He could also "sell" a fake better than anyone. Many times Pelé scored into wide-open goals because the keeper had just dived to stop a shot he thought Pelé would take—but didn't! Pelé was a genius when it came to faking defenders too. Sometimes a fake got him an open shot, and sometimes it set up a scoring chance for a teammate. Pelé might have been most dangerous when he did not have the ball. If opponents did not watch him carefully, they paid the highest price. He could score in the blink of an eye after receiving a pass. Pelé retired with 1,281 goals. He scored 90 of those for his country during international tournaments, including the World Cup. Brazil won the World Cup in 1958, 1962, and 1970.

Eusebio/Portugal   *1957–1978*

In the years after World War II, many European teams began looking for talent in Africa. They set up soccer schools in their countries' colonial territories. Then they picked the best players to bring north. African players were quick, clever, and very skillful. However, they were often bullied by bigger, more aggressive opponents. The bullying stopped when Eusebio da Silva Ferreira arrived. Eusebio was trained in Mozambique and joined Benfica of the Portuguese League in the late 1950s. For nine years in a row, he was the league's top scorer and one of its toughest players. Teams tried everything—legal and illegal— to stop Eusebio. He was too big to push around, too strong-willed to discourage, and too speedy to control. Eusebio could squeeze off blistering shots with either foot and from many different angles. He led Portugal to the European Cup in 1962 and was the scoring star of the 1966 World Cup. In all, Eusebio scored 38 goals for Portugal in 46 international games.

Rock-solid Eusebio was almost impossible to stop during the 1960s.

Gerd Müller/West Germany 1963–1981

Gerd Müller was nicknamed Der Bomber for his explosive kicks. Time and again, he would get to loose balls near the goal and blast them into the net. Some said he was lucky. Others said he did not have the all-around skills of a true star. The truth is that Müller was the greatest goal scorer of the 1970s. He used his quick wits and tree-trunk thighs to score more than 600 goals in his career. In 14 seasons for Bayern Munich, he scored 365 times. In 62 international games for West Germany, Müller scored 62 times. He also began a tradition in German soccer by looking for opportunities in the chaos around the goal.

George Best/Northern Ireland 1963–1984

George Best looked like a member of the Beatles.

Soccer in the United Kingdom was a "working class" game until George Best came along. With his amazing skill and rock-star lifestyle, Best turned the sport into a new form of entertainment. During the 1960s, his fans called the mop-top superstar the fifth Beatle. Millions of fans began watching soccer because of Best's remarkable play. At a time when passing and shooting made up most attacks, Best was a fantastic one-on-one dribbler. He practically screwed opponents into the ground as he changed direction and darted through the defense. When it came to finishing with a great shot, few players in history were better. Best played most of his career with Manchester United. He scored more than 200 goals.

Johann Cruyff/Netherlands 1964–1984

Johann Cruyff was a goalkeeper's nightmare. He could turn up anywhere, with the ball on his foot and a clear shot at the net. Cruyff had the talent and intelligence to play any position on the field. And often he did. This was part of the Dutch system of "Total

Football." In this style of play, teammates exchanged roles as they followed the flow of the game. Cruyff's skill and unpredictability made him one of the greatest scoring threats in the world.

Michel Platini/France   1972-1987

The midfielder in Italian soccer is expected to think defense first. Michel Platini disagreed. He could launch a rush on the opposing defense with a great pass or join the attack as a striker. Platini used his powerful shot and great imagination to win European Footballer of the Year three times during the 1980s. He was World Footballer of the Year in 1985. Platini played much of his career in the Italian League with Juventus. He was a skilled defender, but he also scored 68 goals in 147 league games.

Diego Maradona/Argentina   1976-1997

Diego Maradona was the best player in the world during the 1980s. He was a master at creating something out of nothing. Maradona's secret was his build. He was short, thick, and played low to the ground. He could change direction or take a shot faster than opponents could move to stop him. He was also too strong to be bumped off the ball. The only way to control Maradona was to surround him. But this was a risky strategy. Besides being a great scorer, Maradona was an even better passer. When opponents left his teammates open, it was almost like giving up a free goal.

Michel Platini

Marco Van Basten/Netherlands   1982–1993

During the late 1980s and early 1990s, Marco Van Basten was the best goal scorer on the planet. His kicks were like laser beams—fast, straight, and right on target. Van Basten was an excellent athlete, but his mind was his greatest weapon. He saw plays develop before the defense did. Sometimes it seemed to him the game was moving in slow motion—but he was still going at full speed. Opponents often had no choice but to foul Van Basten. Unfortunately, this caused a serious ankle injury that ended his career. Van Basten was named European Footballer of the Year three times from 1988 to 1992.

Michelle Akers/United States   1984–2000

Michelle Akers combined size, strength, and toughness to become the first great player in U.S. women's soccer. When she was in position for a header, no one in the world could stop her. Akers had a powerful shot and great stamina. At the end of games, she was the most dangerous player on the field. Akers was the first American woman to play pro soccer. She used this experience to dominate the 1991 Women's World Cup.

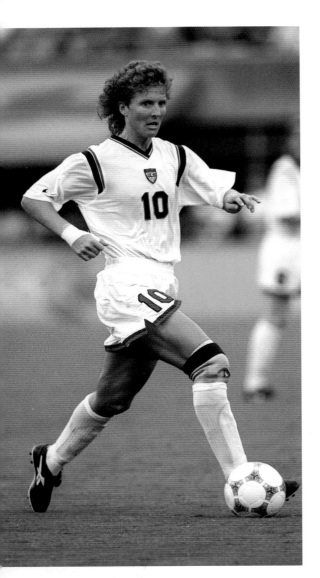

Michelle Akers

Mia Hamm/United States   1987–2004

Which player scored more international goals than anyone in history? Mia Hamm, who retired with 158 in 275 games. Hamm joined Team USA at the age of 15. By the age of 19, she was the team's best player. Hamm was a swift and powerful forward who swerved around defenders without breaking stride. When she was within striking distance of the goal, there was no one better. With her square jaw and piercing eyes, Hamm sent opponents into a panic—and then calmly waited for an opening before booting the ball through. For every goal Hamm scored on a great pass or a thrilling run, she blasted one through a tangle of bodies at point-blank range. She was always in the right place at the right time. Hamm led the United States to two World Cup championships and two Olympic gold medals. She also was an amazing college player. She appeared in 95 matches for the University of North Carolina and scored 103 goals. The Tar Heels lost only one game with Hamm on the field.

Zinédine Zidane/France   1988–2006

Many players try crazy new ways of scoring during practice. Zinédine Zidane was one of the only players who would actually come up with these ideas during games. He mixed talent, strength, and imagination like no one else in soccer. When Zidane was on the field, no lead was safe. He could score goals or create them for teammates with his amazing moves. In 2002 Zidane proved himself a great leader when he carried France to victory in the World Cup. He scored 95 goals as a pro and another 31 for his country in international matches. Each one was memorable in its own way.

Ronaldo/Brazil   1993–Present

At the age of 18, Ronaldo Luís Nazário de Lima was scoring a goal a game against the best defenses in the world. Few finishers have ever been so good so young. Ronaldo has the feet of a dancer and the body of a boxer. When opponents try to poke the ball away, he dribbles around them as if the ball were connected

Ronaldo

to his foot by a string. When they try to bump Ronaldo off the ball, they just bounce off him. His combination of speed, skill, and strength has made him one of the most feared scorers in soccer for more than ten years.

David Beckham/England   1993–Present

David Beckham combines a powerful leg with great creativity to make a soccer ball do strange and wonderful things. Because his kicks reach speeds close to 100 miles (160 kilometers) per hour, goalkeepers tense up when he is within striking distance. This is when Beckham has the most fun. He can kick a ball that starts in one direction and curves sharply in the opposite direction. If a keeper does not read the spin, he has no chance of stopping the shot. Beckham's greatest talent is taking free kicks. When opponents set up a defensive wall between him and the goal, he can bend the ball around them so that it curves sharply into the goal. When fans watch Beckham's goals on video, some almost look fake!

Ruud van Nistelrooy/Netherlands   1993–Present

Ruud van Nistelrooy began his career as a central defender for a Dutch soccer team. He uses his knowledge of how to stop goals to become a top scorer himself. In 2001 he joined the great British club, Manchester United. In 2002–2003, van Nistelrooy scored 44 goals in 52 games for ManU. He can sense when defenders have made a mistake, and he has the talent to make them pay. He can score on short tap-ins, long booming shots, headers, and penalty kicks.

Thierry Henry/France   1994–Present

Speed is the key to Thierry Henry's game. There is not a player in the world who can outrun him once he reaches full gallop. It is not much easier stopping Henry one-on-one. He is a great dribbler who only needs to gain a step before he explodes past his man. When Henry is eye to eye with a goalkeeper, he uses a strong and accurate shot to finish what he started. No wonder opponents admit that they have nightmares when they are getting ready to play Henry's team.

Ronaldinho/Brazil
1998–Present

Ronaldinho celebrates a goal.

As a boy, Ronaldo de Assis Moreira reminded his friends of the great Ronaldo, so they nicknamed him Ronaldinho (Little Ronaldo). He played mostly on the beach until his teenage years. When he moved to a proper field, his game took off. Ronaldinho does things with his feet and body that no one has ever seen before. He takes shots and makes passes sideways and upside down. He quickly became the soccer world's most celebrated "artist." Ronaldinho is a fearless attacker from midfield, from the wing, or as a striker.

Abby Wambach/United States   1998–Present

No goalkeeper is safe when Abby Wambach is near. She is an expert at stealing passes and winning balls in the air. She is especially good at headers. Wambach scored an amazing goal for Team USA to beat archrival Norway 1–0 at the 2003 Women's World Cup. In 2004 her header in extra time won the Olympic gold medal for the United States. Wambach proved her toughness at the 2007 Women's World Cup when she needed 11 stitches to close a gash in her head in the opening game. She went on to score six goals in six games for Team USA.

Landon Donovan/United States   2001–Present

U.S. Soccer has been training young players since the 1980s. The program's best goal scorer is Landon Donovan. He has great speed and moves and can score with either

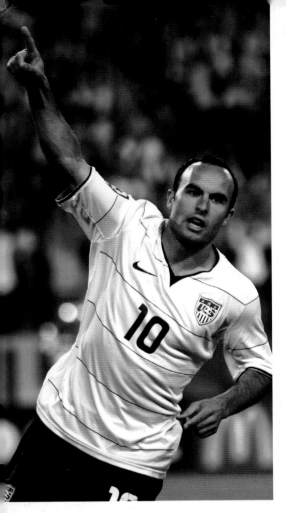

Landon Donovan

foot. Few Americans have the skill to create their own goals one-on-one, but this is Donovan's specialty. He led the San Jose Earthquakes to the Major League Soccer Cup in 2001 and 2003 and won another MLS Cup with the Los Angeles Galaxy in 2005. In 2008 he teamed with David Beckham and Edson Buddle on the Galaxy and scored 20 goals in 25 games. He scored his 100th goal at the age of 25.

Marta/Brazil   2002–Present

Marta Vieira da Silva—or Marta as she is known throughout soccer—was named World Player of the Year in 2006, 2007, and 2008. At the 2007 Women's World Cup, she won the Golden Boot Award as the top scorer. She also won the Golden Ball Award as the tournament's best player. In the semifinal against the United States, Marta scored one of the wildest one-on-one goals ever seen. The lightning-quick midfielder relies on a hard, accurate shot. But she is at her best when dribbling through and around defenders. Marta showed both on her amazing play against the United States.

Lionel Messi/Argentina   2004–Present

The soccer world took notice when Diego Maradona announced that Lionel Messi was his "successor." Like Maradona, Messi can dribble through entire defenses to score goals. He can also set up teammates with pinpoint passes. Messi became a top pro at 16. He soon moved to Europe to join FC Barcelona. There he teamed with Ronaldinho to produce some of the most beautiful goals ever seen in the Spanish League. Messi scored his first World Cup goal at 18. In 2008, at the age of 21, he was voted the world's best player in an online poll of soccer fans.

4 Did You See That?

AMAZING GOALS AND GOAL SCORERS

Every goal, in its own way, is amazing. For one player to outwit and outkick 11 others is quite an accomplishment. This is true whether the game is being played in a backyard with Mom watching or in a stadium filled with 120,000 crazed fans. Some goal-scoring feats, however, are truly incredible. When you see them or read about them, your mouth hangs open in disbelief.

For jaw-dropping goals, no one was better than Pelé. He first made his mark during the 1958 World Cup, when he was just 17. Pelé's goal against Sweden in the final is his most famous. But in an earlier game against Wales, he scored in almost exactly the same way. With the score tied 0–0, Pelé controlled a pass with his chest, popped the ball in the air with his thigh, spun around a defender to face the goal, and then kicked the ball in before it touched the ground. Brazil won 1–0.

Pelé is also remembered for scoring goals on bicycle kicks. There are many pictures of him upside down, with his head near the ground and his foot kicking the ball high in the air. Although he tried this amazing shot many times, he only remembers scoring four or five goals this way. Pelé learned the bicycle kick as a

David Beckham

boy from coach Waldemar de Brito. He had played on Brazil's national team in the 1930s with Leonidas da Silva—the player credited with inventing this shot.

Leonidas was the greatest name in Brazilian soccer during Pelé's childhood. But Leonidas's most famous goal did not come on an acrobatic kick. During the opening round of the 1938 World Cup, Brazil faced Poland. Both teams were known for their attacking style. Heavy rain had made the field sloppy, but the players had no trouble scoring goals. Brazil won 6–5. The story of the game was Leonidas, who scored one of the goals barefoot. Frustrated by his mud-caked shoes, he took them off and played as he had as a child. When the Poles protested, the referee made Leonidas put his shoes back on.

David Beckham is another player whose most famous goal was not a result of his "specialty." Beckham is known for his mastery of the free kick. However, there was nothing "free" about the shot he tried on opening day of the 1996–1997 season. Beckham's Manchester United club was beating Wimbledon 2–0 late in the game. Beckham had the ball at midfield, along the right touchline. He looked up to see goalkeeper Neil Sullivan standing a bit too far in front of the goal line. Beckham booted a long, twisting lob that caught Sullivan by surprise. The poor keeper tried to retreat and make the save. But Beckham's shot was absolutely perfect. It curled into the net from 60 yards away.

Sometimes it takes more than superhuman skill to score an amazing goal. Occasionally, it also takes superhuman strength. The Brazilian striker Ronaldo is often compared to a National Football League running back. He showed why in a 1998 Spanish League game against Santiago de Compostela. Ronaldo, the star of FC Barcelona, dribbled past five players on a thrilling 40-yard run. The last

Saving Grace

When the discussion turns to amazing goals, don't forget about amazing goalkeepers. In a sport that is all about teamwork, keepers are the "loners" on the field. As the only players who can use their hands, goalkeepers are expected to keep the ball out of the net at all times.

When keepers are under attack, they must calculate all the odds. They must play all the angles. They must know the skills of their opponents, plus the strengths and weaknesses of their own players. On top of being the "thinkers" on the field, they must also be acrobats. When a shot comes screaming toward the goal, they must launch their bodies into the air to stop it. When they make a save, it is something to see. When they don't, they are the loneliest people on the field.

Soccer fans will argue forever who scored the greatest goal. There are many candidates. However, when it comes to the greatest save, most agree. It came during the 1970 World Cup. England was playing Brazil. Goalkeeper Gordon Banks (*right*) had his hands full that day. The Brazilians moved the ball quickly all over the field.

Ten minutes into the game, Banks spotted trouble brewing. Carlos Alberto sent a crisp pass down the right side to Jairzinho. The speedy winger slipped past one defender. Banks moved over to protect the right post. Jairzinho did not shoot. Instead, he flicked the ball over Banks's teammates, directly onto the head of Pelé, who was closing in on the goal. Pelé outjumped Tommy Wright and headed a low, hard shot just inside the left post.

The instant Banks saw Jairzinho's pass go across the penalty area, he began moving toward the opposite post. As Pelé headed the ball, Banks hurled his body through the air. Pelé saw nothing but net and shouted "Goal!" But then Banks came, flying toward the post. He stretched as far as he could and managed to get his thumb on the shot—and deflect it up and over the bar. Pelé, the scorer of more than 1,000 goals, described the save as the best he'd ever seen.

defender tried to wrap his arms around Ronaldo and throw him to the ground. The young star dragged the defender a few yards and then blasted the ball past the helpless goalkeeper.

A remarkable goal often starts with a remarkable pass. In fact, most well-known "finishers" owe at least a part of their fame to crisp-passing teammates. The greatest example of this was probably Esteban Cambiasso's goal in the 2006 World Cup. It came in a game between Argentina and the team from Serbia and Montenegro. The Argentines used 21 passes to work the ball into scoring position—then they really went to work! Juan Román Riquelme fed Javier Saviola, a feared scorer. Saviola quickly slipped the ball to Cambiasso. Cambiasso spotted Hernan Crespo, another sharpshooter, cutting toward the goal and knocked the ball ahead to him. As the defense moved toward Crespo, he backheeled the ball to Cambiasso, who drilled it past the goalkeeper for an unforgettable score.

Many soccer fans believe that for a goal to be truly amazing, it must come under pressure. If this is true, then the goals scored by Italy against Czechoslovakia in the 1938 World Cup final are the most amazing ever. Before the match, Italian dictator Benito Mussolini sent the team a telegram. It said, "Win or Die." This was a popular saying in Italy at the time, but the players were worried that Mussolini might have been serious. They beat Hungary 4–2 and lived to play another day. The Hungarian goalkeeper was sad to have lost, but he said he was proud to have saved 11 lives.

Sometimes it is not the quality of goals that is amazing. It is the quantity. When Brazilian star Ronaldinho was a boy, he was a fantastic beach soccer player. He once scored every goal in a 26–0 victory. Of course, this happened at a very low level of competition.

As a rule, the better the players, the harder it is to score goals. During the 1920s and 1930s, England was home to the world's best soccer. Many games ended 0–0 or 1–0. Yet every once in a while, a player would produce a flurry of goals that would leave everyone in the stadium stunned.

The Italian national team waves to the crowd during the 1936 Olympics. Two years later, the team was told "Win or Die!"

Most everyone has heard the old saying, "You can't win 'em all." However, when one player scores seven goals, that team should win the game. In 1922 Wilf Minter of St. Albans knocked in every one of his team's goals in an FA Cup contest against Dulwich. Early in the first half, Minter tapped in a ball that rebounded off the crossbar. He also scored on a header and on a give-and-go with a teammate. In the second half, he tapped in another rebound off the post and then beat the keeper on two hard shots. The score was tied 6–6 after 90 minutes. In extra time, Minter tipped in a corner kick. However, Dulwich scored twice. When the final whistle blew, the score was Dulwich 8 and Wilf Minter 7!

In 1930 John Dyet of King's Park scored eight goals in a 12–2 victory over Forfar Athletic in a Scottish League game. The jubilant King's Park fans had one question: who is John Dyet? They knew Gilbert Dyet, the team's halfback. Well, John was his little brother. After the King's Park star center forward was injured the

He's a Keeper

During the 2008 Major League Soccer season, the New York Red Bulls unexpectedly lost their goalkeeper. They needed a replacement in a hurry. They signed Danny Cepero (*left*), a college player who lived nearby. Two days later, Cepero was in the net against the Columbus Crew. Late in the game, the Crew was whistled for a foul near the Red Bulls' goal. The referee placed the ball on the ground, and Cepero decided to take the kick.

Cepero sent a long, high ball toward the Columbus goal. It traveled much farther than anyone expected. The Columbus keeper froze. He could not decide whether to race out and stop Cepero's kick or retreat to his own net and catch it on a bounce. The ball bounced in front of the keeper and high over his head and into the goal. Cepero's goal was the first ever by a keeper in the MLS history. Not bad for his first day on the job!

day before, young John was pressed into action—it was his first game! After his eight-goal debut, King's Park signed him up.

Six years later, another newcomer had a record-setting game. Joe Payne was a benchwarmer for Luton Town. When he did see action, it was at halfback or wing. But for a game against the Bristol Rovers, Payne had to step in for the team's two center forwards. Both were injured. Ninety minutes later, England had a new superstar. Payne, a former coal miner, scored 10 times against Bristol. Two years later, he was one of the highest-paid players in the country and a member of the national team.

Luton Town was the victim in another goal-scoring storm, in 1961. In pouring rain on a muddy field, Denis Law of Manchester City scored six goals in just over an hour. Law's double hat trick came in a game when most of the other players could barely stay on their feet. The more he scored, the harder it rained. Finally, after 69 minutes, the referee called off the game.

5 A Little Help!

THE WEIRDIST, WILDEST GOALS IN SOCCER HISTORY

The soccer rule book limits teams to 11 players on the field at a time. The book also says that everything on the field is in play. Not surprisingly, some of soccer's strangest goals have occurred when something extra—either human or animal—gets involved. Indeed, having a "12th man" can make all the difference when a game hangs in the balance.

In soccer, where every goal is precious, referees play an especially important role. A game can be won or lost on one poor decision. But what happens when a ref becomes part of the action? Consider the story of referee Ivan Robinson. In a 1968 match in the United Kingdom, he "scored" a goal—and it turned out to be the game winner! Robinson was in the right place but at the wrong time. He was about 20 yards from the net when a shot by George McLean of Barrow came screaming at him. Robinson jumped over the ball, but it ticked the inside of his left foot—just enough to change the direction of McLean's shot and fool the keeper. The final score was 1–0.

In a 1995 match between two German clubs, a referee named Klaus Hartwig was standing outside the goal area watching the action in front of the net. A player took a shot that missed badly and hit Hartwig in the forehead. The ball bounced past the bewildered goalkeeper. The goal counted and tied the score 1–1. The game was delayed while doctors used ice on the gigantic lump rising from Hartwig's head.

Taking a goal away from a team can be even more dangerous for a referee. In a 1998 match in Italy between Castel San Pietro Terme Calcio and Rimini Calcio, fans blamed referee Antonio Marini for "stealing" a goal from Rimini with his bad calls. The game ended in a 1–1 tie. Marini soon realized the fans weren't leaving the stadium, which meant he wasn't either. Finally, police had to call in a helicopter to get Marini out of town safely!

Not every strange goal takes place at the top levels of soccer. In fact, one of the wildest occurred during a youth league game in England in the 1990s. A 13-year-old boy named Danny Worthington took a shot from 25 yards and then quickly turned away in disgust. He thought he had booted the ball too high. When he turned back, he was amazed to see the ball in the goal—and a stunned seagull on the field trying to regain its wits. Worthington's shot had struck the bird in the head, and the ball ricocheted past the keeper. The referee allowed the goal, and the seagull flew off unhurt.

Moon Over Paris

During the 1938 World Cup, Italian superstar Giuseppe Meazza (*below, left*) took a penalty kick against Brazil. It had been a very rough match. Meazza's shorts had been torn during the game, but he ignored this as he blasted the ball toward the net. Unfortunately, the force of the kick destroyed what was left of his uniform. When Meazza looked down, his pants were in tatters around his ankles!

COUPE DU MONDE 1938

Flying creatures have played a role in other unusual goals. A 1992 match in Argentina between Regional and Estudiantes was interrupted by the strange sight of four parachutists floating into the stadium. They had been blown off course and were looking for a safe place to land. As they fell to the earth, an Estudiantes player picked up the ball. The referee called him for a hand ball. Because the violation occurred in the penalty area, Regional was awarded a penalty kick. They made it and won the game.

Many games have been disrupted by dogs running loose on the field. A few goalkeepers have even been chased out of the net by canines with a point to prove. And there are taller tales to tell. For instance, in the 1890s, one of the most popular "athletes" in the sport was a soccer-playing elephant. The creature's name has been lost to history, but it belonged to a circus owner named Sanger. The elephant could kick penalty shots with an oversized ball and also stop shots kicked by humans!

On a trip through England, Sanger challenged the pro team in Leicester to a contest. Three players lost to the elephant. The team's last hope was the fourth player, William Keech. He battled the pachyderm to a 2–2 tie. They played again, and this time, Keech won 3–2. He scored his goals by faking the elephant to one side of the net and then booting the ball the other way—three times! Who said elephants never forget?

Knockout Game

Scoring goals can be dangerous work. Sometimes a player must risk pain and injury to get the shot he wants. In other cases, the goal is the easy part. It's the celebration that will get you! During the 1954 World Cup, Uruguay's Juan Hohberg scored a goal with four minutes left against Hungary. It tied the score at 2–2. Hohberg's teammates were so overjoyed that they knocked him unconscious during the celebration. A groggy Hohberg woke up in time to play the extra period. He hit the crossbar with a shot, and Uruguay lost the match.

6 For the Record

WORLD CUP GOAL-SCORING RECORDS

Soccer
World Cup Scorers

coring a goal in the World Cup is the ultimate achievement in soccer. Each country brings its top players to the tournament. When you put the ball in the net, it means you've succeeded against the very best. These are the players and teams that made history on the biggest stage of them all.

PLAYERS—MEN

Most Goals

In a Tournament	13	Just Fontaine (*top left*)	France, 1958
In a Final	3	Geoff Hurst	England, 1966
In a Game	5	Oleg Salenko (*bottom left*)	Russia, 1994

Most Hat Tricks—3 Goals in a Game

2	Gabriel Batistuta	Argentina, 1994 and 1998
2	Gerd Müller	West Germany, 1970
2	Just Fontaine	France, 1958
2	Sandor Kocsis	Hungary, 1954

All-Time World Cup Scorers—through 2006

15	Ronaldo	Brazil
14	Gerd Müller	West Germany
13	Just Fontaine	France
12	Pelé	Brazil
11	Jürgen Klinsmann	Germany
11	Sandor Kocsis	Hungary
10	Gabriel Batistuta	Argentina
10	Gary Lineker	England
10	Miroslav Klose	Germany
10	Helmut Rahn	Germany
10	Teófilo Cubillas	Peru
10	Grzegorz Lato	Poland

PLAYERS—WOMEN

Most Goals

In a Tournament	10	Michelle Akers	USA, 1991
In a Final	2	Michelle Akers	USA, 1991
In a Game	5	Michelle Akers	USA, 1991

Hat Tricks—3 Goals in a Game

Carolina Morace	Italy, 1991	Sun Wen	China, 1999
Michelle Akers	USA, 1991	Inka Grings	Germany, 1999
Carin Jennings	USA, 1991	Mio Otani	Japan, 2003
Kristin Sandberg	Norway, 1995	Sandra Smisek	Germany, 2007
Ann-Kristin Aarones	Norway, 1995	Birgit Prinz	Germany, 2007
Pretinha (*above right*)	Brazil 1999	Ragnhild Gulbrandsen	Norway, 2007
Sissi	Brazil, 1999		

All-Time Women's World Cup Scorers—through 2007

14	Birgit Prinz (*above*)	Germany		9	Hege Riise	Norway
12	Michelle Akers	USA		9	Abby Wambach	USA
11	Sun Wen	China		8	Liu Ailing	China
11	Bettina Wiegmann	Germany		8	Mia Hamm	USA
10	Ann-Kristin Aarones	Norway		8	Kristine Lilly	USA
10	Marta	Brazil		8	Marianne Pettersen	Norway
10	Heidi Mohr	Germany		7	Tiffeny Milbrett	USA
9	Linda Medalen	Norway		7	Sissi	Brazil

TEAMS

Most Goals—Men

ALL TIME	202	Brazil
IN A TOURNAMENT	27	Hungary, 1954
IN A FINAL	5	Brazil, 1958

Most Goals—Women

ALL TIME	84	Germany
IN A TOURNAMENT	25	USA, 1991 • Germany, 2003
IN A FINAL	2	USA, 1991 • Norway, 1995 • Germany, 2003 and 2007

7 Back of the Net

THE FUTURE OF THE GOAL

During the past 30 years, new technology and training methods have made soccer more exciting than ever. Soccer shoes (or "boots") are lighter, stronger, and more flexible. They give goal scorers more power and control, no matter what condition the field is in. Soccer balls also hold up better. In the old days, a wet field made the ball heavy and hard to shoot. The modern ball is the same from the beginning of a match to the end.

The players are stronger and faster than they were a generation or two ago. They are in better condition, they have more stamina, and they recover from injuries faster. Advances in sports medicine and nutrition have also helped to make players better than ever.

Cristiano Ronaldo is big, strong, and fast. Players with his talent will always be among the world's top scorers.

Lionel Messi (*left*) flies high in the air for a scoring opportunity. He is dangerous around the goal because of his quickness and creativity. There will always be room in soccer for goal scorers like him.

Soccer also continues to benefit from its worldwide popularity. It's hard to find a corner of the globe where the sport isn't played. In the United States, children are introduced to the game every day. The same is true in countries everywhere else on the planet. The imagination and creativity that kids and teenagers bring to soccer is crucial to the sport's growth. By watching their favorite stars and then putting their own spin on the game, young players can discover new ways to score goals. Of course, they also may discover new ways to stop goals.

Are goals any easier to score than in the past? Will it be easier to score in the future? The answer to both questions is no.

That is the beauty of soccer. Even though the goal scorers are better, so are the defenders and goalkeepers whose job it is to stop them. Soccer, remember, is a game of two halves. For every play one team tries, the other team is ready to react. Every goal is truly the result of wonderful teamwork and great individual effort.

Resources

Websites

The FA   http://www.thefa.com

The official site of the Football Association, the governing body for amateur and professional soccer in England, including the Premier League and the FA Cup, features information on teams and players plus statistics and history.

FIFA   http://www.fifa.com

The official site of the Fédération Internationale de Football Association, the international governing body for men's and women's soccer, includes information and statistics on men's and women's professional soccer around the world. FIFA organizes most of the world's major international soccer tournaments, including the World Cup.

JockBio   http://www.jockbio.com

The Web's most comprehensive biographical sports site features profiles of the top soccer players, plus a daily list of their birthdays.

MLS   http://www.mlsnet.com

The official site of Major League Soccer, the governing body for professional men's soccer in the United States, features information on teams and players plus statistics and history.

NCAA   http://www.ncaa.com

The official site of the National Collegiate Athletics Association features information on both the men's game and the women's game at the college level, including statistics and history.

WPS   http://www.womensprosoccer.com

The official site of Women's Professional Soccer, the governing body for professional women's soccer in the United States, features information on teams and players plus statistics and history.

Books

- Cloake, Martin. *Soccer: The Ultimate Guide.* New York: DK Publishing, 2008.
- Coleman, Lori. *Play-By-Play Soccer.* Minneapolis: First Avenue Editions, 2000.
- Crisfield, Deborah W. *The Everything Kids' Soccer Book: Rules, Techniques, and More about Your Favorite Sport!* Cincinnati: Adams Media Corp, 2009.
- Gifford, Clive. *The Kingfisher Soccer Encyclopedia.* Boston: Kingfisher, 2006.
- Morris, Chris. *Soccer: From Beckham to Zidane.* New York: Aladdin Books, 2008.
- Rutledge, Rachel. *Women of Sports: The Best of the Best in Soccer.* Minneapolis: First Avenue Editions, 2000.

Index

Page numbers in italics refer to illustrations.

Aarones, Ann-Kristin, 59, 60
Ailing, Liu, 32, 33, 60
Akers, Michelle, *14*, 44, *44*, 59, 60
Alberto, Carlos, 26, 27, *27*, *51*

Bahr, Walter, 18, 19
Ball, Alan, 24
Ballack, Michael, 34
Banks, Gordon, 26, *51*
Batistuta, Gabriel, 58, 59
Beckham, David, 34, 46, 48, 50, *50*
Best, George, 42
Bloomer, Steve, 36, 37
Buddle, Edson, 48
Burruchaga, Jorge, *29*

Cambiasso, Esteban, 52
Carlos, Roberto, 34, 35, *35*
Cepero, Danny, 54
Charles I (king), 7
Charlton, Bobby, 24, 40, *40*
Chastain, Brandi, 32, 33, *33*
Clodoaldo, 26
Crespo, Hernan, 52
Cruyff, Johann, 42
Cubillas, Teófilo, 59
Cunningham, Jeff, *14*

da Silva, Leonidas, 38, 50
da Silva Ferreira, Eusebio, 41
Dasaev, Rinat, 31
Dean, Bill "Dixie," 37, *37*
de Assis Moreira, Ronaldo, "Ronaldinho," 47, 48, 52
de Brito, Waldemar, 50
Diamante Negro, 38, *38*
DiCicco, Tony, *33*
Di Stéfano, Alfredo, 39
Donovan, Landon, 47, *48*
Dorrance, Anson, *14*
Dyet, Gilbert, 53
Dyet, John, 53, 54

Edward III (king), 8
Elizabeth II (queen), *25*

Feola, Vincent, 22
Figo, Luís, 34
Finney, Tom, 18, *19*,
Fontaine, Just, 58, 59
Foudy, Julie, *14*, 32
Friedenreich, Arthur, 37

Gaetjens, Joe, 18, *18*, 19, *19*
Garrincha, 23
Gérson, 26
González, Raúl, 34

Greaves, Jimmy, 24
Grings, Inka, 59
Grosics, Gyula, *20*
Gulbrandsen, Ragnhild, 59
Gullit, Ruud, 30, 31, *31*

Hamm, Mia, *14*, 32, 44, 45, 60
Harkes, John, *14*
Hartwig, Klaus, 56
Hege, Riise, 60
Henderson, Chris, *14*
Henry, Thierry, 46
Herberger, Sepp, 20, 21
Hohberg, Juan, *57*
Hodge, Steve, 28
Hong, Gao, 33
Hurst, Geoff, 24, 25, *25*, 59

Jairzinho, 26, 27, *51*
Jennings, Carin, 59
Jones, Cobi, *14*

Keech, William, 57
Klinsmann, Jürgen, 59
Klose, Miroslav, 59
Kocsis, Sandor, 39, *39*, 58, 59

Lalas, Alexi, *14*
Lato, Grzegorz, 59
Law, Denis, 54
Lilly, Kristine, *14*, 32, 60
Lineker, Gary, 59

Maradona, Diego, 28, *28*, 29, *29*, 43, *43*, 48
Marini, Antonio, 56
Marta. *See* Vieira da Silva, Marta
McLean, George, 55
Meazza, Giuseppe, *56*
Medalen, Linda, 60
Meola, Tony, *14*
Messi, Lionel, 48, *62*
Milbrett, Tiffeny, 60
Minter, Wilf, 53
Mohr, Heidi, 60
Moore, Bobby, 24, *24*
Morace, Carolina, 59
Muhren, Arnold, 31
Müller, Gerd, 42, 58, 59
Mussolini, Benito, 52

Neuville, Oliver, 34

Orsi, Raimundo, 16, *17*
Otani, Mio, 59

Payne, Joe, 54
Pelé, *5*, 13, *14*, 22, *22*, 23, *23*, 26, *26*, 27, *27*, 39, 40, 49, 50, *51*, 59
Peters, Martin, 24, *25*
Pettersen, Marianne, 60
Piola, Silvio, 38
Planicka, Frantisek, 16, *17*
Platini, Michel, 43, *43*
Pozzo, Vittorio, 16
Pretinha, 59
Prinz, Birgit, 59, 60
Puc, Antonin, 16
Puskas, Ferenc, 20, *21*, 39, 40

Rahn, Helmut, 20, 21, *21*, 59
Ramsey, Alf, 24
Rijkaard, Frank, 31
Riquelme, Juan Román, 52
Rivelino, 26
Roberto, Zé, 34
Robinson, Ivan, 55
Ronaldinho. *See* de Assis Moreira, Ronaldo
Ronaldo, 34, 45, *45*, 50, 52, 59
Ronaldo, Cristiano, 61

Salenko, Oleg, 58
Sandberg, Kristin, 59
Sanger, 57
Saviola, Javier, 52
Schiavio, Angelo, 17
Scurry, Briana, 32, 33, *33*
Shilton, Peter, 28, *28*, *29*
Sissi, 59, 60
Smisek, Sandra, 59
Sullivan, Neil, 50

Tostão, 26, *26*
Twellman, Taylor, *14*

Van Basten, Marco, 30, *30*, 31, *31*, 44
van Nistelrooy, Ruud, 46
Vava, 23, *23*
Vieira da Silva, Marta, 48, 60

Wambach, Abby, 47, 60
Wen, Sun, 59, 60
Wiegmann, Bettina, 60
Williams, Bert, *18*, 19
Winterbottom, Walter, 18
Worthington, Danny, 56
Wright, Tommy, 51

Yunjie, Fan, 32

Zidane, Zinédine, 34, *34*, 35, *35*, 45